UNDERSTANDING SEXUAL HARASSMENT

What Managers and Employees Need to Know about Sexual Harassment

A Guide to Sexual Harassment, Retaliation Claims, and Investigations for Managers, Supervisors, Employees, and Union Representatives

Joseph Swerdzewski

Copyright © 2020 by Joseph Swerdzewski

All rights reserved. This book, or parts thereof, may not be reproduced in any form without written permission from the author/publisher.

Printed in the United States of America
First Edition Printed 2020

ISBN:	978-0-9910121-7-6
Written by:	Joseph Swerdzewski
Edited by:	Jessica Hope Jordan
Cover design by:	Nina Soden
Layout by:	Nina Soden
Published by:	Joseph Swerdzewski

ATTENTION CORPORATIONS, UNIVERSITIES, COLLEGES, AND PROFESSIONAL ORGANIZATIONS: Quantity discounts are available on bulk purchases of this book for educational, or training purposes. Special books or book excerpts can also be created to fit specific needs.

FOR MORE INFORMATION ABOUT
UNDERSTANDING SEXUAL HARASSMENT
Books and/or Learning Materials for Organizations
1-256-503-2226
Joseph Swerdzewski
6585 Highway 431 South
Suite E 457
Hampton Cove, AL 35763

Table of Contents

Introduction 1

Chapter 1. What is Sexual Harassment? 3

Chapter 2. Types of Sexual Harassment 8

Chapter 3. Retaliation 12

Chapter 4. How Employees File A Charge of Sexual Harassment 16

Chapter 5. How to Respond to Sexual Harassment and Retaliation Claims 19

Chapter 6. How to Investigate Sexual Harassment and Retaliation Complaints 22

Chapter 7. The Investigator 28

Chapter 8. How to Interview Sexual Harassment and Retaliation Witnesses 34

Chapter 9. How to Make Credibility Determinations in Sexual Harassment and Retaliation Cases 43

Chapter 10. How to Determine and Effect Confidentiality Requirements When Conducting Sexual Harassment and Retaliation Investigations ... 47

Chapter 11. How to Devise and Effectuate Corrective Actions Against Employees Found to Have Engaged in Sexual Harassment as well as Prevent Future Sexual Harassment 49

Chapter 12. Examples of Best and Worse Practices for Handling Sexual Harassment and Retaliation Complaints and Investigations 54

Chapter 13: How Much Have You Learned? 56

~ Understanding Sexual Harassment ~

Introduction

With the advent of the Me Too movement, sexual harassment has moved to center stage in several workplace disputes. However, sexual harassment as a violation of law existed long before the Me Too movement. The law hasn't changed as a result of this newer movement; however, an increased awareness of the right for employees to complain about sexual harassment has. Sexual harassment has always been wrong, but what has changed is that, today, employees may not be as reluctant to raise a claim as in the past.

For this reason, this guide illuminates specifically what can be considered workplace sexual harassment. Unfortunately, many managers still do not fully understand what sexual harassment is and how it affects employees in the workplace. For example, many managers do not know that sexual harassment occurs not only between men and women, but can also occur between persons of the same sex. Beyond providing a full explanation of what sexual harassment is, this guide further demonstrates how managers should investigate and respond to claims of sexual harassment. It additionally provides an understanding of sexual harassment for employees who may be affected by it.

First, it is important to note that sexual harassment has several deleterious effects on workers who are either victimized by or exposed to it. Those who are subjected to sexual harassment often experience emotional and physical symptoms for years following the events. The effect of these symptoms can have a major impact not only on the lives of those directly affected, but also on workplace productivity. Sexual harassment affects all workers, and its true cost includes:

- Decreased Productivity
- Increased Turnover

- Reputational Harm
- Decreased Morale
- Thousands of Dollars in Settlements and Judgements

A tense or hostile environment due to sexual harassment has an impact on performance, which further affects the ability for an employer or team to fulfill their purpose. Absenteeism and tardiness may rates go up, while employees may stop giving their best and make more mistakes.

Importantly, understanding sexual harassment is not just about staying out of trouble, but also truly valuing all employees in the workplace, regardless of gender. A good manager therefore needs to know how certain actions may be perceived in order to ensure that all employees have a workplace where they are valued for what they contribute, and where they are not demeaned or treated inappropriately because of their gender.

Chapter 1. What is Sexual Harassment?

Sexual harassment is a form of sex discrimination that violates Title VII of the Civil Rights Act of 1964. Title VII applies to employers with 15 or more employees, including state and local governments. It also applies to employment agencies and labor organizations, as well as to the federal government. The law forbids discrimination when it comes to any aspect of employment, including hiring, firing, salary, job discrimination in terms of reassignments, promotions, layoffs, training, fringe benefits, and any other terms or condition of employment. (Appendix A – Sexual Harassment Regulations)

According to the U.S. Equal Employment Opportunity Commission (EEOC), sexual harassment can occur in a variety of ways:

- The victim, as well as the harasser, can either be a man or a woman—a victim does not have to be of another gender.

- The harasser may be the victim's supervisor, an agent of the employer, a supervisor in another area, a co-worker, or a non-employee, such as a vendor or customer.

- The victim does not have to be only the person being harassed but could also be anyone affected by the offensive conduct.

- Unlawful sexual harassment may occur without economic injury to, or discharge of, the victim.

- The harasser's conduct must be unwelcome.

Harassment can include "sexual harassment" or unwelcome sexual advances, requests for sexual favors, and other verbal or physical harassment of a sexual nature.

This includes physical, verbal, or non-verbal conduct of a sexual nature, such as:

- Unwanted sexual attention
- Sexual advances
- Requests for sexual favors
- Sexually explicit comments
- Other conduct of a sexual nature

To be considered sexual harassment, the behavior does not always have to be of a sexual nature. It can also include offensive remarks about a person's gender. For example, it is illegal to harass a woman by making offensive comments about women in general.

Sexual harassment may be direct or implied and committed by an individual who knows, or reasonably should know, that such conduct is unwanted and offensive. Such conduct can often be considered as

- Hostile
- Threatening
- Derogatory
- Demeaning
- Abusive
- Intended to insult, embarrass, belittle, or humiliate

Forms and Locations of Sexual Harassment

Sexual harassment can occur in many ways and places. The following are some examples (which should not be considered an inclusive list of prohibited behaviors):

Physical - This not only includes overt, intrusive actions, such as assault or other forms of physical abuse, but also includes more covert actions, such as touching others in areas that are not generally considered appropriate. Passing by someone in the workplace and touching their shoulder might not in and of itself be considered inappropriate physical contact; however, consistently engaging in this behavior could meet the definition of inappropriate contact.

Verbal - This can include disparaging remarks about a person's gender, comments and/or jokes of a sexual nature, requests for sexual favors, or unwelcome sexual advances.

Visual or Non-Verbal - These can include facial expressions, suggestive gestures, leering, or be verbal, such as making sounds or whistling. These can further include displaying or sharing sexually suggestive media in paper or electronic form.

Online or Electronic - Sexual harassment can occur anywhere, such as online or through other electronic platforms. This can include sharing sexually suggestive comments or media through posts in social media platforms, or emailing, texting, and calling, etc.

Offsite – This includes work-related social events, business travel, or unwelcome visits to a person's home or hotel room.

Examples of Sexual Harassment

Examples of conduct that could be considered sexual harassment:

Denying **an Employment Benefit** - Denying (directly or indirectly) an employment benefit or employment-related opportunity to an employee for refusing to comply with a sexually-oriented request.

***Threatening* Denial of an Employment Benefit** - Threatening (directly or indirectly) to deny an employment benefit or an employment-related opportunity to an employee for refusing to comply with a sexually-oriented request.

***Providing or Promising* an Employment Benefit** - Providing or promising (directly or indirectly) to provide an employment benefit or employment-related opportunity to an employee in exchange for complying with a sexually-oriented request.

***Engaging* in Physical Contact** - Engaging in sexually explicit or suggestive physical contact, including touching another employee in a way that is unwelcome or restricts an employee's movement.

***Displaying or Transmitting* Pornography** - Displaying or transmitting pornographic or sexually oriented materials, such as photographs, posters, cartoons, drawings, or other images, or storing or accessing such materials on government-owned equipment or employer-owned equipment for personal use or consumption.

***Engaging* in Indecent Exposure or *Exposing* Body Parts to Attract Sexual Attention**– Engaging in indecent exposure of body parts usually kept private in order to attract sexual attention. Exposing body parts to attract sexual attention could include a low-cut blouse or tight pants.

***Making* Obscene Gestures** – Making obscene gestures of a sexually-oriented nature.

***Making* Romantic Advances** – Making romantic advances toward an individual and persisting, despite rejection of the advances.

***Using* Sexually Oriented Language** – Using sexually-oriented language or making sexually-related propositions, jokes, or remarks, including graphic verbal commentary about an individual's body or clothing.

***Sending* Sexual Messages** – Sending sexually suggestive or obscene messages by mail, in person, telephone, text, or any other electronic communication.

Although the law doesn't prohibit simple teasing, offhand comments, or isolated incidents that do not form a pattern of conduct, harassment in the workplace is illegal when it is so frequent or severe that it creates a hostile or offensive work environment, or when it results in an adverse employment decision (such as the victim being fired or demoted).

Chapter 1 Key Points:

1. Sexual harassment is a form of discrimination.
2. It is unlawful to harass a person because of a person's gender.
3. Both victim and harasser can be a man or a woman, and the victim and harasser can be of the same gender.
4. The harasser can be the victim's supervisor, a supervisor in another work area, or someone who is not an employee of the employer, such as a client or customer. The harasser can also be a co-worker, even though liability may not attach unless the employer was aware of and allowed the harassment.

Chapter 2. Types of Sexual Harassment

Most managers understand that asking for sexual favors is considered sexual harassment. However, beyond a direct quid pro quo, sexual harassment can also be considered the establishment of a hostile work environment. What follows compares these two types of sexual harassment:

Quid Pro Quo: This legal term means making a victim's submission to unwelcome sexual advances, or their submission to other verbal or physical conduct of a sexual nature, a term or condition of their employment. Basing employment decisions on the victim's submission to, or rejection of, such conduct is considered quid pro quo sexual harassment. In other words, unwelcome sexual advances, requests for sexual favors, or other conduct of a sexual nature is quid pro quo sexual harassment when:

Hostile Environment: This occurs when making unwelcome sexual advances or other verbal or physical conduct of a sexual nature with the purpose of, or that which creates the effect of, unreasonably interfering with an individual's work performance, or creating an intimidating, hostile, or offensive working environment.

To be unlawful, the conduct must create a work environment that would be intimidating, hostile, or offensive to reasonable people.

Offensive conduct may include, but is not limited to, offensive jokes, slurs, epithets or name calling, physical assaults or threats, intimidation, ridicule or mockery, insults or put-downs, offensive objects or pictures, and interference with work performance. Harassment can occur in a variety of circumstances.[1]

In addition to the person who is directly sexually harassed, other employees who are impacted by the harassment (by hearing or viewing it) are also considered victims. They, too, may then find the work environment intimidating or hostile, and this may affect their work performance as well. In this manner, harassers can affect many more people than just the targeted employee.

Unlawful hostile work environment must be claimed by someone who is a part of *a legally protected class*. Under the law protected classes include gender, race, nationality, religion, disability, sexual orientation, age, and sex. Once it is determined that an employee is part of a legally protected class, the conduct must further be defined as both *pervasive and abusive*. In doing so, lawyers seek to show that the average reasonable human being would find the conduct hostile and abusive.

From a legal standpoint, hostile actions further take into account the following concerns:

- Frequency

---

[1] This book is specifically about sexual harassment; however, it is also important to understand that other forms of harassment that might not be considered sexual harassment may still be a violation of law. As aforementioned, today, considerable emphasis is being placed on sexual harassment in the workplace. However, this focus on sexual harassment in the workplace should not lead to a failure to deal with harassment for other prohibited behaviors. For both managers and employees, it important to recognize that a hostile work environment can also exist when unwelcome comments or conduct based on gender, race, nationality, religion, disability, sexual orientation, age, or other legally protected characteristics unreasonably interfere with an employee's work performance or create an intimidating or offensive work environment for not only the employee who is being harassed, but also for others. These types of conduct can also severely diminish an employee's productivity as well as their self-esteem.

- Severity
- Physically Threatening
- Work Performance Interference
- Psychological Effects
- Harasser's Position in the Workplace

Each case of sexual harassment is analyzed on a case-by-case basis. The type of behavior, the specific complaint, the frequency and severity, as well as the above-mentioned criteria, are all considered. There is no set formula for determining sexual harassment; however, where unwanted physical contact is involved, it is more likely, based on the nature and frequency of that contact, to be considered sexual harassment.

As aforementioned, quid pro quo cases may be considered sexual harassment when linked to the granting or denial of employment benefits. Nevertheless, the conduct would have to be considered severe for a single incident or isolated incidents of offensive sexual conduct or remarks to rise to the level of a hostile environment. Unlike quid pro quo claims of harassment, hostile environment claims usually require proof of a pattern of offensive conduct. However, a single, severe incident of quid pro quo sexual harassment, such as fondling or aggressive physical touching, may be enough to constitute a Title VII violation. A general rule of thumb is that the more severe the harassment is, the less likely it is that the victim will be required to demonstrate a repetitive series of incidents. This is especially true when the harassment is physical, such as unwanted touching.

Chapter 2 Key Points:

1. There are two types of sexual harassment: Quid pro quo and hostile environment.
2. A hostile work environment is a workplace in which unwelcome comments or conduct of a sexual nature unreasonably interfere with an employee's performance or create an intimidating or offensive work environment.
3. Each case of sexual harassment is analyzed on a case-by-case basis

Chapter 3. Retaliation

Anti-discrimination laws also prohibit harassment against individuals in retaliation for filing a discrimination charge, testifying, or participating in any way in an investigation, proceeding, or lawsuit, or opposing employment practices that they reasonably believe discriminate against individuals.

The EEO laws prohibit punishing job applicants or employees for asserting their rights to be free from employment discrimination, including sexual harassment. Asserting these EEO rights is called "protected activity," and it can take many forms. For example, it is unlawful to retaliate against applicants or employees for:

- Filing or being a witness in an EEO charge, complaint, investigation, or lawsuit.
- Communicating with a supervisor or manager about employment discrimination, including harassment.
- Answering questions during an employer investigation of alleged harassment.
- Refusing to follow orders that would result in discrimination.
- Resisting sexual advances or intervening to protect others.

Engaging in EEO activity, however, does not shield an employee from all discipline or discharge. Employers are free to discipline or terminate workers if motivated by non-retaliatory and/or non-discriminatory reasons that would otherwise result in such consequences. However, an employer is not allowed to do anything in response to EEO activity that would discourage someone from resisting or complaining about future discrimination.

For example, it could be considered retaliation if an employer takes action because of an employee's EEO activity by doing any of the following:

- Reprimanding the employee or giving a performance evaluation that is lower than it should be.
- Transferring the employee to a less desirable position.
- Engaging in verbal or physical abuse.
- Threatening to make, or making, reports to authorities (such as reporting immigration status or contacting the police).
- Increased scrutiny
- Spreading false rumors, treating a family member negatively (for example, canceling a contract with the person's spouse).
- Making the person's work more difficult (for example, punishing an employee for an EEO complaint by purposefully changing their work schedule to conflict with family responsibilities).

Retaliation occurs when an employer takes a materially adverse action because an individual has engaged, or may engage, in activity in furtherance of the EEO laws. Each of the EEO laws prohibits retaliation and related conduct.

A retaliation claim that challenges an action taken because of EEO-related activity has three elements:

(1) **Protected activity**: "participation" in an EEO process or "opposition" to discrimination;

(2) **Materially adverse action** taken by the employer; and

(3) Requisite level of **causal connection** between the protected activity and the materially adverse action.

In a large number of EEO cases, it is common for an original discrimination allegation (on a basis other than retaliation) to fail to establish a violation of the law; however, the subsequent retaliation allegation results in an adverse finding.

The finding of retaliation is common because individuals often seek to avenge a perceived offense. The desire to retaliate is a common human reaction, but when committed by a management official because an employee is asserting their right to challenge a perceived wrong, the retaliation can then establish a legal liability.

Some examples from past cases can provide instructive illustrations of typical retaliatory behavior:

> In a recent case, an employee who had filed several unsuccessful EEO complaints subsequently sought promotions within the organization. The employee learned, however, that her manager had placed information about the previous EEO proceedings in her personnel file as well as communicated that the employee had filed several complaints when the manager was contacted for reference checks. The EEOC found that the statements made during the reference checks were retaliatory, and that the EEO information placed in the employee's personnel file was unnecessary, and thus hindered her promotional opportunities.
>
> Similarly, another recent case involved an employee who claimed that she was discriminated against during the promotional interview process. Two of the three interview panelists were managers involved in current or previous EEO complaints by the employee, and one of the panelists attempted to influence the selection process by asking a question that paralleled a previous conflict between the panelist and the employee. A witness reported that he had heard the manager make the statement, "I don't get mad; I

get even," in reference to employees who make discrimination claims. The EEOC found that the selection process was tainted by retaliatory conduct and ordered the agency to promote the employee.

Chapter 3 Key Points:

1. Retaliation against individuals for filing a discrimination charge, testifying, or participating in any way in an investigation is a violation of law.
2. It is common for an original discrimination allegation (on a basis other than retaliation) to fail to establish a violation of the law, but for the subsequent retaliation allegation to result in a finding of liability.
3. There must be a causal connection between the protected activity and the retaliatory action claimed.

Chapter 4. How Employees File A Charge of Sexual Harassment

The processes employees use to file a charge of sexual harassment discrimination are different for private sector employees and the federal sector. While the law regarding sexual harassment is the same for both federal sector and private sector employees, the processes for filing a charge of discrimination for each type of employee must be followed closely to ensure compliance with all regulatory and statutory requirements.

In the private sector, a charge of discrimination is a signed statement asserting that an organization engaged in employment discrimination. It requests that the Equal Employment Opportunity Commission (EEOC) take remedial action. Any employee filing a charge should look at the information provided by the EEOC on its website. (www.eeoc.gov) The laws enforced by EEOC require an employee to file a charge first before they can file a lawsuit for unlawful discrimination. There are strict time limits for filing a charge. Where the discrimination took place can also determine how long an employee has to file a charge. The EEOC 180-calendar-day time limit for filing a charge may be extended based on the state and locality where you live.

Private sector employees may file charges in person at an EEOC office, by mail, or online using the EEOC Public Portal. Charges may also be filed at a State or Local Fair Employment Practice Agency. If an employee has any questions about the process, they should feel free to call the EEOC office nearest them. (Appendix B – Filing a Formal Complaint)

If you are a federal employee or job applicant, and you believe that a federal agency has discriminated against you, you have a right to file a complaint. The first step is to contact an EEO Counselor at the agency where you work or where you applied for a job. Generally, you must contact the EEO Counselor within 45 days from the day the discrimination occurred or the date you became aware of the discrimination. In most cases the EEO Counselor will give you the choice of participating either in EEO counseling, or in an alternative dispute resolution (ADR) program, such as a mediation program. (Appendix C – Federal EEO Complaint Processing)

If you do not settle the dispute during counseling or through ADR, you can file a formal discrimination complaint against the agency with the agency's EEO Office. You must file within 15 days from the day you receive notice from your EEO Counselor about how to file. Once you have filed a formal complaint, the agency will review the complaint and decide whether the case should be dismissed for a procedural reason (for example, your claim was filed too late).

If the agency doesn't dismiss the complaint, it will investigate. The agency has 180 days from the day an employee filed a complaint to finish the investigation.

When the investigation is finished, the agency will issue a notice providing two choices: either request a hearing before an EEOC Administrative Judge or ask the agency to issue a decision as to whether the discrimination occurred.

The discrimination complaint process does not prohibit either private sector or federal sector employees from discussing a complaint about sexual harassment with a manager. Most employees are reluctant to file formal charges of discrimination, but instead hope to have their complaints handled without resort to litigation. For many employees, a formal EEO process is their last resort for resolving sexual harassment issues. However, employees should realize that reporting harassment or discrimination to a manager does not toll the time limits for initiating a complaint.

Chapter 4 Key Points:

1. It is important for employees to follow the required processes for pursuing a charge of sexual harassment.
2. A charge of sexual harassment that is not timely filed may be dismissed.
3. A private sector employee filing a charge should contact EEOC with any questions about the process.
4. A federal sector employee should contact their agency's EEOC office if they have any questions about the process.

Chapter 5. How to Respond to Sexual Harassment and Retaliation Claims

When a claim of sexual harassment is received by a manager or supervisor, the way in which it is handled matters greatly for both the employer and the employee. If improperly handled, it can have a major impact of the employee's trust in the management of the organization as well as may create an even greater liability on the part of the employer.

An employee usually finds it very difficult to make allegations about sexual harassment or discrimination. They worry about the consequences and the effect the complaint will have on others in the workplace. They may even feel both vulnerable and concerned about losing their job.

The employer should therefore show respect, understanding, and concern, including during the initial responses to the complaining party. Employees and managers may have misbehaved and violated employer standards, and the complainant may be legitimately upset and concerned about that behavior. Swift and appropriate action, including thanking the employee for raising the concern as well as quick initiation of an investigation, sends a message not only to the complaining employee, but also to others watching for the employer's reaction.

Employees who observe the employer taking concerns seriously are more likely to seek internal resolution and less likely to resort to litigation.

When receiving such a complaint the manager/supervisor should be mindful of the following:

- Employees do not have to use "magic" words such as "harassment" when making a claim that warrants employer action, so managers must understand the concern well enough to determine whether the issue should be treated as an allegation of harassment or hostile work environment.

- The first thing is Do NOT ignore it. Once someone comes forward to a manager, the employer is now "on notice." Being on notice creates legal liability for the employer's actions, particularly if nothing is done about a legitimate claim. The manager receiving the claim should listen and take the issue seriously, be professional, and nonjudgmental. The manager is not supposed to determine the validity of the complaint, but rather only to gather enough facts to be able to forward the matter for investigation. The manager should contact the Human Resources office to be advised of the employer's protocol when an employee talks with a manager about a claim of sexual harassment.
- Resist making statements that imply a judgment or position such as: "maybe he or she didn't mean it," "maybe you should not dress that way," or "maybe you should not have responded the way you did."
- Assure that the "victim" is aware of available employer resources, such as counseling services.
- Assure that the "victim" is aware anonymity cannot be guaranteed.
- Ask the "victim" if he or she would like to be temporarily moved to a different location (or telework) during pendency of investigation.
- Assure that the "victim" is aware of his or her right to seek redress through formal processes, such as a union grievance or EEO complaint.

The manager should find out what offices need to be involved and make contact as soon as practicable, as the EEO, Security, and/or Human Resources, etc. may need to be involved.

When briefing others on the initial complaint, assure that you use a "need to know" approach. In other words, which offices need to know about the complaint, and what information do they need to know. Managers in the chain of command of the alleged bad actor may also need to know that an investigation will be occurring as well as the nature of the allegation, but they likely do not need to know all the details of the allegation. A briefing based on a need to know basis will protect them from accusations of pre-judging a situation (especially if these managers may end up participating later as a proposing or deciding official). When putting anything in writing about the complaint, be aware of the possibility that any written document could be discoverable.

Chapter 5 Key Points:

1. The initial contact between manager and an employee claiming sexual harassment can hold great significance for the employee.
2. The very first things a manager should understand when an employee brings a claim of sexual harassment is not to ignore the claim, or to try in any way to minimize the significance of the claim.
3. Briefing others on a claim should be done on a "need to know basis."

Chapter 6. How to Investigate Sexual Harassment and Retaliation Complaints

The employer should promptly investigate complaints (including those which initially appear to be meritless). Failure to treat a complaint seriously can significantly exacerbate the problem and increase the liability. Investigations of these concerns should be conducted by persons with training and experience who can be both neutral and impartial (i.e., who don't report to or have relationships with those individuals involved in the complaint and do not have a preconceived bias for one side or the other). In most cases, the investigation is not done by a supervisor, but rather someone in the EEO office or by a contractor. It is important that supervisors understand what takes place during an investigation, and how the investigation is conducted, because of the impact an investigation can have on the workplace.

The purpose of an investigation is to develop a record and provide a decision-making tool; no judgments should be made during the investigative process. The investigator's job is not to make a decision, but rather to establish the facts. In investigating a complaint, the investigator should consider the following:

1. In planning the investigation, the investigator should determine who might be in the role of final decider if the evidence later shows discipline is warranted as well as assure that this individual is only given status updates during the investigation (versus any details).

2. Assure the complaining party at the outset that the complaint will be treated seriously, that there will not be any retaliation for raising the complaint, and that any concerns about retaliation should be brought to the

investigator's attention immediately so that they can be addressed.

3. Instruct the accused not to contact the complainant regarding the complaint, and not to engage in conduct that is—or may be viewed as—retaliatory. And, if the accused violates the instructions (which can happen), take action immediately.

4. The investigator needs to keep an open mind when gathering and reviewing information, and to refrain from coming to a conclusion until all relevant data has been collected, reviewed, and assessed.

5. Parse the complaint to determine the scope of the investigation and specific nature of the concern(s); stay focused on the scope of the harassment/retaliation complaint, and do not turn the investigation into a general workplace assessment.

6. Understand the legal definitions of "sexual harassment" and "retaliation" to know the elements of proving such a case. Here are some examples of the elements of hostile environment sexual harassment:
   - The employee must be a member of a statutorily protected class;
   - The employee was subjected to harassment in the form of unwelcome verbal or physical conduct involving that protected class;
   - The harassment complained of was based on employee's statutorily protected class;
   - The harassment affected a term or condition of employment and/or had the purpose or effect of unreasonably interfering with the work environment

and/or creating an intimidating, hostile, or offensive work environment; and
- There is a basis for imputing liability to the employer (it is fair to find the employer liable; they were on notice of the conduct and did nothing, etc.).

7. Understand the standard of preponderance of the evidence (known as "more likely than not"). The evidence must show that, more likely than not, the harassment or retaliation took place.

8. Review available documents first, such as policies and documents submitted with the complaint, etc. In general, the investigator should try to learn as much as they can about the issues before reaching out to start interviews.

9. Determine a witness list with the idea of only interviewing people with direct knowledge of the event(s) in question; the witness list can be expanded as information develops.

10. Each interview should be consistent in the topics covered but may differ for various reasons. For example, not every witness may need to know who the "victim" and "accused" parties are, depending on the circumstances, in order to provide relevant information.

11. Each interviewee should be advised not to share the substance of his/her interview with anyone.

12. Interviewees should be asked if they know of anyone who has direct knowledge of the facts. However, witnesses should not be told who is being or will be interviewed. Interviewees should also be asked for relevant documents.

13. Be watchful for facts that could create new issues. For example, any suggestion of child pornography could have criminal implications. In such cases, the investigation should halt until appropriate contacts and releases are obtained.

14. Determine union involvement. If there is a union in the workplace, it may have rights to observe or otherwise participate in the investigation.

15. Given that most employers will not discipline an employee with "sexual harassment," be less concerned with whether the behavior at issue meets the strict definition of sexual harassment and more concerned with whether the conduct was inappropriate.

16. Constantly assess the evidence being gathered—is it, or can it be, verified?

17. Get signed statements from witnesses. As this is not a criminal investigation, employees cannot refuse to participate in the investigation.

18. Allow employees to review and make corrections to their statement but instruct them that edits should be for accuracy purposes only, and not to "say things better."

19. Assure that there is a way to track employee edits.

20. Consider whether follow-up interviews (at least with the "victim" and alleged harasser) are necessary to flesh out contradictions and/or inconsistencies.

21. Consider the "product" that should be provided at the end of the investigation, especially as it pertains to any kind of summary report.

22. Consider how to deal with any personally identifiable information in the record— should it be redacted? How will it be secured?

Many employers prefer essentially no investigative report and want the evidence (the statements and documents gathered) provided, given that reports are discoverable. If a report is generated, only a factual recitation should be provided, unless otherwise requested by the employer.

It is management, not the investigator, who must assess the evidence and make their own judgments on the credibility of the complaint and the weight of evidence, etc., to decide what actions (if any) should be taken. However, some employers want the investigators to make recommendations, or even conclusions as to whether harassment or retaliation occurred. If no report is requested, the employer may consider a briefing by the investigator.

Here are some tips for an appropriate investigation:

- Determine the appropriate scope of the investigation; the scope will vary depending upon the allegations and should be reassessed if the facts change.

- Choose an investigator who has good people skills and judgment; both qualities will be important in almost every investigation. If you don't have a qualified neutral candidate inside, hire an experienced one from outside.

- If the initiation of the investigation is delayed (for example, because the appropriate internal investigator is traveling, or the employer is searching for an appropriate outside investigator), document the reasons for the delay. The employer may need to explain in litigation, possibly years down the road, why it did not begin to investigate immediately.

- The investigator should coordinate activities with legal counsel, where appropriate, so that the employer can determine whether the investigation will be privileged. This is especially important for the drafting of memos or notes associated with the investigation.

Chapter 6 Key Points:

1. The employer should promptly investigate complaints.
2. The purpose of an investigation is to develop a record and provide a decision-making tool; no judgments should be made during the investigative process.
3. Chose an investigator who has good people skills and judgment.
4. The investigator needs to keep an open mind when gathering and reviewing information, and to refrain from coming to a conclusion until all relevant data has been reviewed and assessed.

Chapter 7. The Investigator

The selection of an investigator is an important part of the handling of sexual harassment and retaliation complaints. The person selected must be considered by the complaining employee and the employees to be a neutral investigator who can conduct an unbiased investigation. Investigators can either be on the staff of the employer or come from outside the organization.

The investigator's authority must be established. What the investigator is authorized to do as part of the investigation must be clearly understood. Is the investigator's role solely to do factfinding, or is the investigator authorized to make recommendations or conclusions on the findings of harassment or retaliation? Lastly, whether the investigator has authority to act as a mediator to work with parties on potential settlement must be understood both by the employer and the employee complainant.

The investigator must act ethically in the conduct of the investigation. There is no formal code of ethics for investigators such as the canon of ethics which applies to attorneys. The following are some ethical guidelines that should be followed by the investigator:

1. The investigator shall observe, and adhere to, the precepts of honesty, integrity, and truthfulness.

2. The investigator shall be truthful, diligent, and honorable in the discharge of their professional responsibilities.

3. An investigator shall provide ethical services within the limits of the law.

4. An investigator shall safeguard confidential information and exercise the utmost care to prevent any unauthorized disclosure of such information.

One of the most important rules for investigators is not to prejudge the outcome of an investigation, and then investigate to prove the preordained conclusion. This does a disservice to both parties because all the relevant facts would not be discovered since the investigation is tilted to either one party or the other. This appearance of bias further discredits the entire investigation. Moreover, the failure to find all the facts may lead to the wrong decisions being made, which can lead to time-consuming, expensive litigation as well as a lack of confidence in the investigation by the employees in the workplace.

A Good Investigator Must:

1. Be prepared. Winston Churchill once said: "Failure to prepare is preparing to fail." The need to prepare before beginning an investigation is an essential part of a good investigation. Preparation includes:
    a. Understanding the issue to be investigated. Understanding the issue includes knowing the elements of the violation of law. As aforementioned, there are discreet elements that must be met to prove sexual harassment. The investigator must know these elements and plan to obtain evidence that either proves or disproves them.
    b. Research applicable law, contract provisions, or technical issues.
    c. Gather and review all available background information. As an example, if the witness has documents that were provided to the EEO Office or his or her manager, these should be reviewed by the investigator before beginning to investigate.
    d. Establish a preliminary list of witnesses. This witness list may be amended, as more information is known, but a good list should be prepared before any testimony is taken.

~ Understanding Sexual Harassment ~

    e. Prepare a list of documents to be obtained that are necessary to the investigation. Documents can be essential in proving or disproving arguments made by either side in the dispute.

    f. Prepare a schedule of potential witness interviews. Preparing a schedule can save wasted time waiting for witnesses to be located and brought to the interview room. In general, the complaining witness should be interviewed first, and the accused should be interviewed last.

2. Be a Good Listener and Able to Evaluate Responses. Investigation is not just taking verbatim notes of what is said by a witness, but more importantly asking the right questions to elicit information that proves or disprove the elements of sexual harassment or retaliation. Be prepared to ask questions necessary to the investigation. Do not simply be a note taker for witnesses' testimony. Understand what you are there to achieve and the best way to achieve it.

3. Establish Rapport with Witnesses. Time spent in establishing a rapport with the witness is paid back in the quality and depth of information received from a witness who trusts the investigator.

4. Maintain Self-Control during Interviews. Shouting at witnesses and berating them may make good TV but has no place in a sexual harassment investigation.

5. Be Objective in your Approach. The more objectivity you project, the more information the witness will be willing to provide.

6. When questioning witnesses, start with open-ended questions, such as "What happened next?" and "Tell me about the meeting," to allow the witness to tell his or her

story, and then follow-up with specific questions to assure you elicit complete information.

7. Exhibit Honesty and Integrity. Witnesses who don't trust the investigator are not as forthcoming with evidence. Investigators develop a reputation in the workplace. A reputation for honesty and integrity makes for a much more effective investigation.

Common Investigatory Problems

There are several common problems investigators encounter that could hinder their investigation. Some of these problems can be corrected with training; others may not be so easily remedied. In some cases, when these become apparent, it may be that the person selected to investigate is not cut out to be an investigator. The following are some of the common problems that investigators may have:

- The investigator is not thorough enough. An investigation is not thorough enough when it does not answer all the questions necessary for a decision. Failure to complete a thorough investigation is usually a result of lack of preparation. If the investigator does not know what they are looking for in the investigation, it is easy to see why the investigation will not be thorough enough. Another common reason for lack of thoroughness is that some investigators set a low bar on what they think is enough evidence. They may make great leaps from the evidence they have gathered to barely sustainable conclusions.

- The investigator is too thorough and can't come to a conclusion for the investigation. Some investigators go to the opposite extreme. They do not feel comfortable making a recommendation or conclusion without exhaustive evidence. They investigate the issue to death, never being sure that they have enough evidence to support their findings. Their investigations drag on, as they try to tie down every possible issue or factual inconsistency.

- The investigator investigates the wrong issue. Sometimes investigators go off on a tangent and investigate the wrong issue. They investigate issues that will not be helpful or necessary to resolve the actual issue in dispute. This often happens because the investigator has done inadequate research into what issues should be investigated. It is also the responsibility of the decision maker who commissions the investigation to make clear what specific issue is expected to be investigated.

- The investigator is unable to analyze the facts. The ability to analyze the facts and their application to legal, regulatory, policy, or contractual standards is a necessary investigative skill. If the investigator is determining whether there is sexual harassment, they must be able to analyze the facts and apply them to the legal requirements for sexual harassment.

- The investigator's conclusions don't fit the facts found in investigation. The conclusions and recommendations made by the investigator must be based on the facts gathered during the investigation. Making unsupported recommendations lessens the credibility of the investigator and may be evidence of bias. If the facts do not support the recommendations and conclusions made by the investigator, any action based on them may not withstand the scrutiny of an arbitrator or judge.

Chapter 7 Key Points:

1. The choice of the right person to investigate a sexual harassment and/or retaliation claim is an important decision in the handling of the claim.
2. Investigators must act ethically in conducting an investigation.
3. Being prepared to investigate greatly improves the quality of an investigation.
4. Establishing rapport with the witnesses helps to gain the best possible evidence from a witness.

Chapter 8. How to Interview Sexual Harassment and Retaliation Witnesses

There are basically four phases of an investigative interview: 1) Introduction, 2) Developing Rapport, 3) Questioning, and 4) Summarization. Each phase plays an important role in the success of the interview.

Introduction

How an interview begins can have a major impact on the subsequent success of the interview. It is important to note that witnesses do not know what to expect when questioned by an investigator. Many are nervous and uncertain as to what is going to take place. Oftentimes, witnesses are fearful about the impact on their job when they provide evidence that could be viewed as detrimental to their supervisor. It is therefore the job of the investigator to gain the confidence of the witnesses help to allay their fear of testifying.

The first thing investigators should do is introduce themselves and explain their role in the investigation. They should state that are a neutral party seeking to obtain the best information concerning a claim of sexual harassment. The investigator should ask the interviewee their name and where they work to make note of their identity. The witness should be told their name was provided as someone who may have some information that could be helpful in the investigation. The investigator will then tell the employee how the investigation will be conducted.

Developing Rapport

Developing rapport is an important way to gain the trust of a witness; therefore, spending time to build rapport with the witness will be time well-spent. Rapport can be achieved by using certain words, tone, inflection, gestures, facial expressions, and stance, as well as conversation. The purpose of developing rapport is to make it easier for the witness to talk to the investigator. At the beginning of the interview, the investigator asks the witness basic questions, such as "What is your name?" "Where do you work?" "What do you do?" "How long have you worked there?" These are easy questions intended to create an atmosphere where the witness feels free to talk to the investigator. Some small talk about topics such as the weather, the ball game, or the city where the investigation is taking place also are intended to get employees talking about non-threatening subjects. The witness has already been told during the introduction about why they are being questioned; however, at this time, ask the witness if they have any questions before the actual investigation questioning begins.

Questioning

How to question a witness is one of the most important skills an investigator must develop. As discussed above, preparing for an investigation is extremely important. In other words, going into an interview unprepared and "shooting from the hip" can lead to "shooting yourself in the foot." A second interview of a witness does not always lead to the results which could have been achieved when a witness is first interviewed. Questioning involves knowing what questions to ask, listening to the response to a question from the witness, and then, based on the response, asking the next question that either follows up on the witness's answer or takes the interview in a new direction.

Summarization

The last phase of interviewing is summarizing the evidence provided by the witness. In this phase, the investigator puts together, in their mind or on paper, a summary of what the witness said. The summary is then compared with what must be proven in the proof analysis to determine whether more evidence is needed.

Some Dos and Don'ts for an Investigation of Sexual Harassment

- Advise witnesses that the factfinder is a neutral in the process. This must also be proven to the witness through your professionalism and a lack of bias.

- Interview the "victim" first and the accused last. The victim is interviewed first so the investigator can gain an understanding of what is being alleged. The accused is interviewed last because it is important to gain as much information about the alleged harassment or retaliation before asking the accused. Without the information from the victim, the investigator may not know what the important questions to ask are.

- Tell witnesses as much as they need to know to be able to answer questions, but no more than necessary. Sharing too much information may "taint" the witness's testimony by giving them the opportunity to answer in order to buttress or refute the other that has been information has been gathered.

- Ask questions; don't comment. The investigator does not share their personal views of the merits of the claim of harassment or the credibility of witnesses. This can lead to the belief that the investigation is biased.

- While it is fine to use some of the same questions for all witnesses, resist having a "script" of questions; instead, it's better to have an outline of the facts you are trying to understand and verify, and to use that outline to prompt the appropriate questions.

- Try to let the witness tell their story, and then ask questions to fill in missing details.

- Ask the "victim" what they are looking for in terms of a resolution.

- If the accused denies the behavior, ask if he or she knows why they think this accusation would have been made.

- Determine the effect on the victim: Did it frighten, scare, or anger the victim?

- Assure that the full context is developed for each instance of concerning the unwanted behavior (first time, witnesses, time, date, and location).

- Avoid identifying the source of information unless it's necessary for the witness to be able to make a complete response.

- Instead of directing the witness towards certain answers, start with general questioning, such as "Tell me what happened," "Tell me your concern," "What about his or her actions was a problem for you?"

- Ask witnesses to identify persons who they believe have direct knowledge of the issues under investigation (however, do not share the identity or number of witnesses you are speaking with).

- Ask witnesses for documents, such as calendar notations, emails, and/or texts, etc.

- End interviews with catch-all question: "Is there anything else I need to know that is relevant to the issues we have discussed?"

- Advise witnesses that they will not be retaliated against for providing truthful information.

Where to Interview

The physical environment, such as comfort, noise, privacy, distance between interviewer and interviewee, seating arrangement, and territoriality, affects interviews. The interview room should be well-lit, moderately-sized, with a comfortable temperature and ventilation. All communication barriers such as desks, tables, and personal items should be eliminated to the extent possible. Smoking and drink breaks should be controlled by the interviewer.

Interview Guidelines

Here are some interview guidelines to follow when conducting an interview of a witness:

- Greet the person in an appropriate manner. The introduction is an important first step in developing a relationship with the person being interviewed. Showing disdain for meeting can yield a defensive witness.

- Define or state the purpose of the interview. The more the person who is being interviewed knows about why they are being questioned, the more responsive they can be to the questions asked. In addition, this can put to rest the fears of most witnesses.

- Maintain control; don't let the interviewee interview you. Keeping control of the interview is very important. Some employees being interviewed will try to take over the interview by asking the investigator questions. Other times, if the employee has a representative, they will also try to take over the interview by asking questions.

- Try to evaluate each piece of information on its own merits. Different types of evidence have different value in an investigation. Hearsay evidence has less value than evidence heard directly by a witness; however, it is still important to the investigation. Documentary evidence may be more credible than witness testimony. Each piece of evidence should be evaluated on its own merits to determine the weight it should be given in an investigation.

- Maintain strict impartiality and keep an open mind. Being impartial gives the investigator a clearer picture of what happened and provides a better viewpoint to make a judgment on the facts. A prejudiced investigation can lead to mistakes that will show up at a hearing when the third-party hearing officer or judge has an opportunity to review the facts. If an investigator starts an investigation with a predetermined outcome in mind, they may find that outcome: however, the investigation may not withstand scrutiny on review.

- Take your time, don't hurry. A good investigator is not just taking statements from witnesses; they are also thinking about the investigation. Investigators must allow themselves time to think about the evidence they need, the evidence they have already collected, as well as how it effects the issues being investigated. Spend time thinking about what the evidence means.

- Be a good listener. An investigation is not just about asking the right questions, but also about listening to the answers. Answers to questions tell the investigator what needs to be followed up on with more questions and when no more information is needed. Listening also requires watching the witness respond to questions. Body language often tells more about an answer than the words used by the witness.

- Accept the interviewee's feelings. The job of the investigator is to obtain the best evidence available. It is not to change the minds of the people being interviewed. The investigator may not agree with what the witness says. Through questioning, the investigator can challenge the veracity of what a witness has put forth as the facts. However, the investigator must respect the feelings of the witness, even if the investigator doesn't agree with the facts as presented by the witness. Facts can be attacked; however, attacking the feelings of a witness is a personal attack.

- Ensure you understand what the witness is trying to say. An investigator should not just write down what the employee has told them. The role of the investigator is not just to be a stenographer. The role is to understand what the witness is saying, and not just transcribing the words. Using clarifying questions can help the investigator determine the meaning or interest behind what a witness is saying.

- Use appropriate questioning techniques. Use the right questioning technique for the witness being interviewed. For example, starting by cross-examining a witness is usually not the right technique to begin an interview. It immediately puts the witness on the defensive. However, using it later in an interview may be appropriate.

- Do not try to solve the problem during the interview. As noted above, unless the investigator is given authority to engage in settlement efforts, the investigator's role is not to resolve the issues being investigated. Trying to solve the problem may lead to an inadequate investigation because more time is spent trying to resolve the issues than is spent gathering evidence. In addition, the evidence can become confused by settlement efforts because it may be difficult to tell what was factual versus what was purely an assertion during settlement discussions.

- Review the information and notes and make certain the investigator and the interviewee agree on what was said. A review of the investigator's notes with the interviewee will help to assure that the investigator has clearly understood the information provided.

- Sometimes, there will be disputes between what the witness said or thought they said, what the witness wants to change from what they did say, and what the investigator heard. In such circumstances, have the witness sign both their version and a red line version of what that investigator heard.

- Make no promises. It is especially important that the investigator make no promises with respect to the outcome of the investigation. The subject of an investigation, however, may ask what will happen to him or her and what the investigator thinks of the evidence. In most cases, the investigator is not the decision-maker, and therefore any promises made maybe premature and/or inaccurate.

- Extend your appreciation. Always thank the person being interviewed for their time and candor during the interview. It is important to end the interview in a gracious, upbeat manner. Thanking the person being interviewed is a good way to end on a high note.

- Close the interview. Bring the interview to a close with a definite ending point. However, tell all witnesses that further information may be needed, and the investigator may need to talk to the witness again as the investigation progresses. Ending the interview in this manner will not lead to surprises if the investigator needs to talk to the interviewee again to clear up issues as other information is obtained.

Chapter 8 Key Points:

1. How an interview begins can have a major impact on the success of the interview.
2. Spending time to build rapport with the witness will be time well-spent.
3. Interview the "victim" first and the "accused" last.
4. Be a good listener.

Chapter 9. How to Make Credibility Determinations in Sexual Harassment and Retaliation Cases

Finding out who is telling the truth, and who is lying, can be a difficult task. Some witnesses could qualify as professional liars that could mislead anyone. However, most witnesses are not of that caliber. Determining the credibility of witnesses is a difficult part of any investigation. Various things to look for in a witness may be helpful but are not always foolproof ways of determining credibility. Some of the following point to a lack of credibility:

- The story changes (in substantive ways)
- Consistently pausing before providing answers
- A witness who is carefully picking and choosing his or her words
- A witness who adds information that is not requested
- Very general responses
- A witness who becomes defensive
- Direct answers versus lengthy, circuitous responses that circle around the question
- A witness with hidden agendas: does the witness have anything to gain if the outcome goes a certain way?
- A witness who makes substantial changes to his or her written statement versus changes for clarification.
- An explanation or version of events that seems implausible.

However, do not confuse someone who is just very nervous about the process, or how the investigation could affect them, with a witness who is being uncooperative or deceptive.

In the federal sector, investigative bodies often use the Hillen Factors (Hillen *v. Dep't of the Army*, 35 M.S.P.R. 453, 458 (1987) when determining credibility. However, this can also be useful in determining credibility in most administrative investigations, even outside the federal sector. When determining credibility, it can be helpful to look at the following:

(1) the witness' opportunity or capacity to observe the event in question;

(2) the witness' character;

(3) any prior inconsistent statement(s) by the witness;

(4) a witness' bias or lack of bias;

(5) a contradiction of the witness' version of events by other evidence or its consistency with other evidence;

(6) the inherent improbability of the witness' version of events; and

(7) the witness' demeanor.

As aforementioned, an important process for how communication takes place is through body language. Witnesses send unspoken messages by how their body reacts to questions as well as how their body reacts when they present answers. Watching how a witness reacts, and how the witness uses their body either knowingly or unknowingly in answering questions, while not evidence in and of itself, can help the investigator to gain a perspective on the truthfulness of the actual answers given.

The following are some general observations about the body language of truthful witnesses:

- Open, Upright and comfortable
- Aligned frontally to face the interviewer directly
- Leaning forward for interest
- Relaxed, casual, with some nervousness or excitement
- Smooth in changes, with no pattern

The following are some general observations of the body language of deceptive witnesses:

- Slouched in chair
- Unnaturally rigid
- Avoid eye contact
- Fidgety
- Lacking frontal alignment
- Tending to retreat behind physical barriers
- Erratic in changes
- Exhibiting head and body slump

Determining credibility is not an exact science. No individual is always right in determining when someone is lying and when they are telling the truth. However, an investigator must still endeavor to gather facts which give the decider the best opportunity to determine the truth of what has been alleged.

Chapter 9 Key Points:

1. Determining credibility is a difficult part of any investigation.
2. Applying the Hillen Factors may prove useful in determining credibility.
3. Body language can be useful in determining credibility.

Chapter 10. How to Determine and Effect Confidentiality Requirements When Conducting Sexual Harassment and Retaliation Investigations.

Confidentiality is an important aspect of sexual harassment complaint processing. There are several issues relating to confidentiality which occur at various stages of the complaint process. These relate to three concerns: 1) initial confidentiality of the name of the individual making the claim, 2) confidentiality of information provided by either the claimant or the employer, and 3) confidentiality of witness testimony during the investigation.

In the private sector, information obtained from individuals who contact the EEOC is confidential and will not be revealed to the employer until the individual files a charge of discrimination. In the federal sector, employees who contact an EEO Counselor will not have their name disclosed until a formal EEO charge is filed. The aggrieved person should be advised by a federal sector EEO Counselor that their identity will not be revealed unless the aggrieved authorizes them to reveal it, or if they file a formal complaint with the agency.

While the employer will be aware of the details of a claim, the EEOC will not disclose to the public any information it collects during its investigation of the claim. A discrimination victim has the further option of taking the employer to court to address their discriminatory actions and recover damages. Once an employee enters the court system, there is a strong presumption in favor of making the details of the case available to the public.

During the investigation, it must be made certain exactly what information needs to be kept confidential and from whom; for example, does the fact of the investigation itself, or just the substance of it, need to be confidential? Are employees allowed to tell family? Part of ensuring confidentiality in such matters, as aforementioned, include assuring that sensitive information is only being shared on a need-to-know basis.

One common practice, which is followed by most employers, is requiring that each witness sign a document affirming that they will keep the fact and substance of the investigation confidential. Witnesses should also be advised that trying to influence an investigation by sharing or soliciting information about the investigation is potential grounds for discipline. At the beginning of each interview, ask the witness if anyone has shared any information about the investigation with them; the witness' answer should be included in the statement they will sign.

In the federal sector, an agency is required to conduct an administrative inquiry separate from the EEO process if an allegation of harassment or hostile work environment is raised so that the concerning behavior can be addressed before the end of potentially lengthy litigation. A complaining party's identity may need to be disclosed in that process if that is the only means to investigate the allegation.

Chapter 10 Key Points:

1. A claimant cannot be guaranteed anonymity throughout the investigation.
2. Once an EEO claim is filed, the name and essential details of the complaint will be disclosed to the employer.
3. In the federal sector, employees who contact an EEO Counselor will not have their names disclosed until a formal EEO charge is filed, unless, as described above, an administrative inquiry is required to be conducted.

Chapter 11. How to Devise and Effectuate Corrective Actions Against Employees Found to Have Engaged in Sexual Harassment as well as Prevent Future Sexual Harassment

Employers, rather than individuals, are financially liable for sexual harassment in the workplace. This means that, if an employer is found guilty of neglecting to stop or prevent sexual harassment, the employer may face court-ordered penalties. In most cases, accused employees are not personally legally liable for violations under EEOC jurisdiction. However, they may nevertheless face penalties from their employer and/or be liable for civil or criminal penalties under other laws.

It is therefore important for the employer to take appropriate action in cases where sexual harassment has been discovered.

Employer Penalties for Sexual Harassment

Title VII of the Civil Rights Act prohibits sexual harassment as a form of illegal sex discrimination. If an employer is found guilty of failing to stop sexual harassment, the law permits the following penalties:

- **Lost wages**. Payments to recover wages and benefits a victim would have earned from the date of the harassment to the date of the trial or settlement.

- **Future lost wages**. Payments to cover wages and benefits a victim would have earned if there had never been a sexual harassment charge.

- **Compensatory damages**. Payments for emotional pain and anguish.

- **Punitive damages**. Payments to punish the employer.

- **Attorney costs and court fees.**
- **Reinstatement or promotion** for the victim.

Employee Penalties for Sexual Harassment

Title VII requires employers to stop or prevent sexual harassment from continuing to occur. If an employee admits to sexual harassment or is found during an investigation to have engaged in sexual harassment or inappropriate conduct of a sexual nature that may rise to the legal definition of "sexual harassment," an employer may take disciplinary action against the employee. Most employers try to make the punishment proportionate to the seriousness of the offensive behavior.

Penalties against a harasser may include:

- Warning or reprimand
- Transfer or demotion
- Salary reduction
- Suspension or termination
- Training or counseling
- Monitoring

In taking any action against employees found to have engaged in sexual harassment, make certain that any discipline is consistent with the action taken for like offenses. In the federal sector, both the proposing and deciding officials must have thoroughly analyzed the evidence because they will "own" the decided-upon corrective action. Also, in the federal sector one uses the Douglas Factors for determining reasonable penalties. In deciding the penalty, ask the following questions: Was this repeated behavior? Was there physical contact? Was the bad actor a manager? Was this intentional behavior? Was there notoriety? Is the alleged harasser in a position that is held to higher standard, such as a manager or law enforcement?

Remember that just because there is an accusation, there does not have to be a disciplinary or corrective action; let the facts (and not panic or pressure) point to a consequence.

Consider using non-disciplinary methods, such as reassignment or training instead of, or in addition to, disciplinary actions to allow one of the parties to let some time pass and to get things back to "normal."

Remedies for Sexual Harassment

Victims of sexual harassment can recover remedies including:

- Back pay
- Hiring
- Promotion
- Reinstatement
- Front pay (compensates the victim for anticipated future losses)
- Compensatory damages (emotional pain and suffering)
- Punitive damages (damages to punish the employer)
- Other actions that will make an individual "whole" (in the condition she or he would have been in, except for the harassment).

Prevent Harassment

The following is a list of things that can be done to prevent and deal with sexual harassment:

- Establish an effective complaint procedure, and encourage employees to feel comfortable coming to you with any problems they face at work, including any harassment that might occur.

- Create and communicate your Anti-Harassment policy.

- Treat any incident as if it is a court case from the moment it is reported (most importantly, notify your attorney and/or EEO and HR Office right away).

- Quickly investigate any claims that might occur.

- Don't take any action that can be viewed as harming the person making the complaint. For example, don't transfer the complaining party to a worse location in order to separate the parties. Employers should not take action against an accused person for the same reasons. Until misconduct is verified, an allegation is just an allegation.

- Do whatever is necessary to stop the harassment immediately.

- Restore any job benefits that were lost due to the harassment.

- Discipline the person who committed the harassment. If disciplinary action of the harasser is not considered appropriate, document the reasons why.

- Take action to correct past discrimination based on the harassing conduct, if appropriate.

- Painstakingly document the investigation and the steps you took to remedy the violation.

- Recognize your obligation to create and preserve a work environment free from sexual harassment.

- Report any allegations of sexual harassment.
- Supervisors *must* set the tone. Publicize the policy through regular meetings and EEO training activities.
- Seek resolutions and document action(s) taken.
- Even if you feel the complaint is groundless, treat it seriously.

Chapter 11 Key Points:
1. Employers may be financially liable for sexual harassment in the workplace.
2. Discipline for sexual harassment may include anything from warnings to removal.
3. Establish an effective complaint procedure and encourage employees to feel comfortable coming to you with any problems they face at work, including any harassment that might occur.

Chapter 12. Examples of Best and Worse Practices for Handling Sexual Harassment and Retaliation Complaints and Investigations

Here are some good and bad ideas for how to handle sexual harassment and retaliation complaints and investigations:

Bad idea: changing the "victim's" hours, duties, and physical location, etc. without communicating with them and working through interim measures; this can be viewed as retaliation.

Bad idea: focusing on what the victim "wants" or the hype around an accusation versus what the facts show is warranted.

Bad idea: doing something that management "assumes" will be beneficial to the "victim" without asking/communicating with the person (this can lead to retaliation complaints from the "victim").

Good idea: advising witnesses, including the "victim," that he or she will not be advised by the investigator of the outcome of the investigation and whether corrective action was taken due to privacy concerns (i.e., manage expectations).

Good idea: during or after the investigation and separate from the specific complaint under investigation, assess the environment to determine root causes and whether an office-wide refresher training may be warranted.

Good idea: Do not become the "morality police;" instead, assess what the impact is to the workplace.

Good idea: during or after the investigation, assess whether spin-off corrective action is warranted; e.g., a manager was aware of the inappropriate conduct at issue and did nothing to intervene/manage since no one had complained.

The worst practice for management is not having a sexual harassment complaint system in place. There should be an established system and process in place for handling sexual harassment complaints. This process should be well-advertised in the workplace. Management should be trained on what sexual harassment is and how to respond to complaints.

Chapter 13: How Much Have You Learned?

Now that you have read this book, let's see how much you have learned. Take the true/false quiz below on sexual harassment to see how well you remember important points.

Sexual Harassment Quiz

True/False Quiz – Determine whether each statement is either true or false. After you finish the quiz, turn to the following page to review the correct answers to see how you did.

1. An employer will not be liable for sexual harassment committed by managers or supervisors if they not aware of the conduct.

2. It is not unlawful harassment for a manager or supervisor to assign unfavorable work duties only to women.

3. To bring a lawsuit for sexual harassment, a victim does not need to show that he or she suffered a monetary or economic harm, such as being fired or demoted.

4. It is unlawful for a man to sexually harass another man because of his gender.

5. Quid pro quo sexual harassment (e.g., promising more favorable working conditions in return for sex) can be committed by managers, coworkers, and even customers or clients.

6. If an employee does not immediately complain about offensive behavior, the behavior is probably welcome, and thus not harassment.

7. An employee who joins in with sex jokes or sexual banter in the workplace may be a victim of sexual harassment.

8. Abusive behavior aimed at one gender that is not "sexual" in nature (e.g., a supervisor who is constantly rude only to female employees and insults them) can also be considered unlawful harassment.

9. A person who works in an office where sexual harassment occurs, but to whom sexual activity is not directed, may still sue the organization for sexual harassment.

10. A manager's threats to retaliate against a subordinate if he or she refuses sexual advances does not constitute sexual harassment if the threats are never carried out.

11. If a victim of sexual harassment asks a manager or supervisor not to tell anyone about the sexual harassment incident, the supervisor should not take further action.

12. If a supervisor sees that an employee has posted sexually explicit posters in his work area, but no one has complained about them, no further action is required.

13. A supervisor who touches an employee in a sexual manner only one time may be guilty of sexual harassment.

14. If my intentions were good, for example, I meant to compliment someone on how great they looked, then there is no way my conduct could violate the sexual harassment policy.

15. Terms of endearment (honey, sweetie, or darling) may be considered sexual harassment.

16. I can ask a co-worker out on a date.

17. Inappropriate behavior isn't wrong or illegal (i.e., they joke like that with everyone) unless it is intended as sexual harassment.

18. The standard for determining offensive behavior is based upon the beliefs of a reasonable person.

19. Even if an employee gives consent to a supervisor's sexual advances, they can still claim sexual harassment.

20. A delivery person comes to your office daily and often makes inappropriate sexual comments to one of your employees, which the employees tell you about. You have no obligation to do anything since the delivery person is not one of your employees.

Answers to the Quiz on Sexual Harassment
True/False Quiz

1. **False**. An employer may be held liable for quid pro quo sexual harassment without prior knowledge. However, there is more debate on to what extent the employer has knowledge of hostile environment sexual harassment. For example, if tasteless jokes are being made at staff meetings, but no one is complaining, the employer will be held responsible for knowing what the environment was like. It is important that when a sexual harassment complaint is brought to the employer, they must take action to investigate as well as any appropriate action to limit the employer's liability and maintain an effective workplace.

2. **False**. The assignment of unfavorable duties only to women can be viewed as a form of sexual harassment.

3. **True**. There need not be an allegation of monetary loss or economic harm for sexual harassment to be claimed.

4. **True**. A man can sexually harass a man and a woman can sexually harass a woman.

5. **True**. Managers, co-workers, customers, and clients can commit sexual harassment. Co-workers can be found liable for quid pro quo sexual harassment if it can be shown that the employee has control over working conditions affecting the complaining employee.

6. **False**. While it is the best practice for an employee to complain immediately about sexual harassment, the failure to do so does

~ Understanding Sexual Harassment ~

not mean the behavior is welcome, and therefore not harassment.

7. **True**. Even though an employee joins in sex jokes or sexual banter, it does not mean the employee cannot claim sexual harassment. Based on the environment in the workplace, the employee may have felt compelled to engage in such activities.

8. **True**. Using demeaning terms aimed at one gender can be considered sexual harassment. It is illegal to harass a woman or a man by making offensive comments about women or men in general.

9. **True**. When hostile environment sexual harassment exists, an employer does not have to be the subject of the harassment to make a claim of sexual harassment.

10. **False**. The mere threats to retaliate are enough to be considered sexual harassment, even if the threats are never carried out.

11. **False**. Even when an employee asks the manager not to tell anyone about the sexual harassment incident, the manager has an obligation to notify the employer of the claim. The fact that the manager was told puts the employer on notice of the claim and could lead to liability if nothing is done about the claim.

12. **False**. The posting of the posters places an affirmative obligation on the employer to take action, even if no complaint is filed. The posters can be views as establishing a hostile work environment, and by their being posted the employer is on notice of the potential for a sexual harassment complaint.

13. **True**. A single, extremely severe incident of harassment may be enough to constitute a Title VII violation. The incident was

"severe"—meaning that even though it only occurred once, it was so severe that any reasonable person within the protected class would be detrimentally affected in their work and life under the same or similar circumstances.

14. **False**. Although the law doesn't prohibit simple teasing, offhand comments, or isolated incidents that are not very serious, harassment is illegal when it is so frequent or severe that it creates a hostile or offensive work environment. Good intentions are not a defense to sexual harassment.

15. **True**. A hostile work environment is a workplace in which unwelcome comments or conduct based on an employee's gender unreasonably interfere with an employee's work performance or create an intimidating or offensive work environment for the employee who is being harassed. This conduct can severely diminish an employee's productivity and self-esteem both in and out of the workplace. These terms applied to one gender could be viewed by employees of that gender as unwelcome comments.

16. **True**. An employee can ask another employee on a date. However, persistent requests that are denied may lead to a claim of a sexual harassment.

17. **False**. There is no need for a sexual harassment claim to prove the intent to sexually harass. The acts will be judged by whether they constitute sexual harassment, regardless of the intention of the person making the remarks.

18. **True**. In determining whether harassment is sufficiently severe or pervasive to create a hostile environment, the harasser's conduct should be evaluated from the objective standpoint of a "reasonable person."

19. **True**. Consent given at one time does not act as waiver of the right of the employee to claim sexual harassment.

20. **False**. Even if the delivery person is not your employee you have an obligation to respond when the employee tells you of the inappropriate comments.

Appendix A
29 CFR § 1604.11 - Sexual harassment.

§ 1604.11 Sexual harassment.

(a) Harassment on the basis of sex is a violation of section 703 of title VII. 1 Unwelcome sexual advances, requests for sexual favors, and other verbal or physical conduct of a sexual nature constitute sexual harassment when (1) submission to such conduct is made either explicitly or implicitly a term or condition of an individual's employment, (2) submission to or rejection of such conduct by an individual is used as the basis for employment decisions affecting such individual, or (3) such conduct has the purpose or effect of unreasonably interfering with an individual's work performance or creating an intimidating, hostile, or offensive working environment.

1 The principles involved here continue to apply to race, color, religion or national origin.

(b) In determining whether alleged conduct constitutes sexual harassment, the Commission will look at the record as a whole and at the totality of the circumstances, such as the nature of the sexual advances and the context in which the alleged incidents occurred. The determination of the legality of a particular action will be made from the facts, on a case by case basis.

(c) [Reserved]

(d) With respect to conduct between fellow employees, an employer is responsible for acts of sexual harassment in the workplace where the employer (or its agents or supervisory employees) knows or should have known of the conduct, unless it can show that it took immediate and appropriate corrective action.

(e) An employer may also be responsible for the acts of non-employees, with respect to sexual harassment of employees in the workplace, where the employer (or its agents or supervisory employees) knows or should have known of the conduct and fails to take immediate and appropriate corrective action. In reviewing these cases the Commission will consider the extent of the employer's control and any other legal responsibility which the employer may have with respect to the conduct of such non-employees.

(f) Prevention is the best tool for the elimination of sexual harassment. An employer should take all steps necessary to prevent sexual harassment from occurring, such as affirmatively raising the subject, expressing strong disapproval, developing appropriate sanctions, informing employees of their right to raise and how to raise the issue of harassment under title VII, and developing methods to sensitize all concerned.

(g) Other related practices: Where employment opportunities or benefits are granted because of an individual's submission to the employer's sexual advances or requests for sexual favors, the employer may be held liable for unlawful sex discrimination against other persons who were qualified for but denied that employment opportunity or benefit.

Appendix B
Filing a Formal Complaint – Private Sector

If you decide to file a discrimination complaint, you must do so within 15 days from the day you received notice from your EEO Counselor about how to file a complaint. This notice is sent to you after your final interview with the EEO Counselor. You must file your complaint at the same EEO Office where you received counseling. The 15-day deadline for filing a complaint is calculated in calendar days starting the day after you receive the notice. If the 15th calendar day falls on a Saturday, Sunday, or federal holiday, then the last day of the deadline is the next business day. The agency is required to give you a reasonable amount of time during work hours to prepare the complaint. If you feel that you have not been given a reasonable amount of time, contact the agency's EEO Director or EEOC's Office of Federal Operations.

What to Include in the Formal Complaint?

Your discrimination complaint must contain the following:

Your name, address, and telephone number;

A short description of the events that you believe were discriminatory (for example, you were terminated, demoted, harassed);

Why you believe you were discriminated against (for example, because of your race, color, religion, sex (including pregnancy, gender identity, and sexual orientation), national origin, age (40 or older), disability, genetic information or retaliation);

A short description of any injury you suffered; and

Your signature (or your lawyer's signature).

Once Formal Complaint is filed

After your complaint is filed, the agency will send you a letter letting you know it received your complaint. The agency will also review the complaint and decide whether your case should be dismissed for a procedural reason (for example, your claim was filed too late). If the agency doesn't dismiss your complaint, it will investigate it. If the agency does dismiss your complaint, you will receive information about how to

Appendix B – Filing a Formal Complaint

appeal the dismissal. Should the agency dismiss your complaint without an investigation, you have 30 days from the day you receive the agency's dismissal to appeal.

In some cases, an agency will dismiss only part of the complaint and continue processing the rest. In this situation, you must wait until the agency issues its final order on all the claims in your complaint before appealing the partial dismissal.

Investigation of Complaint

The agency has 180 days from the day you filed your complaint to finish its investigation. The investigation may be extended by another 180 days if new events are added to your complaint or if you file new complaints that must be added to your original complaint for investigation. You also have the right to agree to an extension of up to 90 days.

When the investigation is finished, the agency will give you two choices: either request a hearing before an EEOC Administrative Judge or ask the agency to issue a decision as to whether discrimination occurred.

If more than 180 days pass and the agency has not yet finished its investigation, you can wait for the agency to complete its investigation, ask for a hearing, or file a lawsuit in federal district court. Once you ask for a hearing, the complaint will be handled by an EEOC Administrative Judge.

The Role of the Agency Investigator

The role of the agency investigator is to gather information related to your complaint. Agency investigators do not decide your case. Instead, they are responsible for gathering the evidence needed to decide whether you were discriminated against.

Reaching a Voluntary Settlement

At any time during the complaint process, the agency can offer to settle your complaint. You are not required to accept a settlement offer.

If you and the agency settle your complaint, it will be dismissed and no further action will be taken. Both you and the agency will be required to do what you promised to do in the agreement.

Appendix B – Filing a Formal Complaint

If the Agency Does Not Comply with the Settlement

If an agency does not comply in some way with the terms of your settlement agreement, notify the agency's EEO Director. You have 30 days from the day you first learned of the agency's failure to comply to give the EEO Director this notice.

The agency must respond to you in writing to try and settle the conflict. If the agency does not respond, or if you are not satisfied with the agency's response, you can appeal to EEOC's Office of Federal Operations for a decision about whether the agency has complied with the terms of the settlement agreement. You must file your appeal within 30 days from the day you receive the agency's response or, if the agency does not respond, after 35 days have passed from the day you notified the agency's EEO Director of the agency's failure to comply. You must give the agency a copy of your appeal. The agency will then have 30 days to respond.

Representation During the Complaint Process

Although you don't have to be represented by a lawyer during the complaint process, you have the right to have a lawyer if you want one. You can also ask someone who is not a lawyer to represent you, or you can represent yourself. The EEOC will not represent you during the complaint process, and we will not appoint a lawyer to represent you.

Adding New Events to Your Complaint

If new events that you believe are discriminatory take place after you file your complaint, you can add them to your complaint. This is called "amending" a complaint. To amend your complaint, you should write the agency's EEO Office, describe what happened, and ask that the new events be included in your complaint.

After your letter is received, the EEO Office will either add the new events to your complaint or send you to EEO counseling to discuss them with an EEO Counselor. If you are sent to counseling and the matter cannot be settled there, you have the right to file a new complaint that includes the new events. The new complaint will later be combined with the original complaint.

Having More Than One Complaint

Appendix B – Filing a Formal Complaint

If you have more than one discrimination complaint against an agency, the agency's EEO Office must investigate your complaints together. This is to ensure that they are investigated as quickly and as efficiently as possible. The EEO Office will notify you before the complaints are combined.

Appendix C
Federal EEO Complaint Processing Procedures

Contact EEO Counselor

Aggrieved persons who believe they have been discriminated against must contact an agency EEO counselor prior to filing a formal complaint. The person must initiate counselor contact within 45 days of the matter alleged to be discriminatory. 29 C.F.R. Section 1614.105(a)(1). This time limit shall be extended where the aggrieved person shows that: he or she was not notified of the time limits and was not otherwise aware of them; he or she did not and reasonably should not have known that the discriminatory matter occurred; despite due diligence he or she was prevented by circumstances beyond his or her control from contacting the counselor within the time limits. 29 C.F.R. Section 1614.105(a)(2).

EEO Counseling

EEO counselors provide information to the aggrieved individual concerning how the federal sector EEO process works, including time frames and appeal procedures, and attempt to informally resolve the matter. At the initial counseling session, counselors must advise individuals in writing of their rights and responsibilities in the EEO process, including the right to request a hearing before an EEOC administrative judge or an immediate final decision from the agency following its investigation of the complaint. Individuals must be informed of their right to elect between pursuing the matter in the EEO process under part 1614 and a grievance procedure (where available) or the Merit Systems Protection Board appeal process (where applicable). The counselor must also inform the individuals of their right to proceed directly to court in a lawsuit under the Age Discrimination in Employment Act, of their duty to mitigate damages, and that only claims raised in pre-complaint counseling may be alleged in a subsequent complaint filed with the agency. 29 C.F.R. Section 1614.105(b)(1).

Counseling must be completed within 30 days of the date the aggrieved person contacted the agency's EEO office to request counseling. If the matter is not resolved in that time period, the counselor must inform the individual in writing of the right to file a discrimination complaint. This notice ("Notice of Final Interview") must inform the individual that a

Appendix C – Federal EEO Complaint Processing

complaint must be filed within 15 days of receipt of the notice, identify the agency official with whom the complaint must be filed, and of the individual's duty to inform the agency if he or she is represented. 29 C.F.R. Section 1614.105(d). The 30-day counseling period may be extended for an additional 60 days: (1) where the individual agrees to such extension in writing; or (2) where the aggrieved person chooses to participate in an ADR procedure. If the claim is not resolved before the 90th day, the Notice of Final Interview described above must be issued to the individual. 29 C.F.R. Section 1614.105(e), (f).

When a complaint is filed, the EEO counselor must submit a written report to the agency's EEO office concerning the issues discussed and the actions taken during counseling. 29 C.F.R. Section 1614.105(c).

Alternative Dispute Resolution (ADR)

Beginning January 1, 2000 all agencies were required to establish or make available an ADR program. Such program must be available for both the pre-complaint process and the formal complaint process. 29 C.F.R. Section 1614.102(b)(2). At the initial counseling session, counselors must advise individuals that, where an agency agrees to offer ADR in a particular case, the individual may choose between participation in the ADR program and EEO counseling. 29 C.F.R. Section 1614.105(b)(2). As noted above, if the matter is not resolved in the ADR process within 90 days of the date the individual contacted the agency's EEO office, a Notice of Final Interview must be issued to the individual giving him or her the right to proceed with a formal complaint.

Complaints

A complaint must be filed with the agency that allegedly discriminated against the complainant within 15 days of receipt of the Notice of Final Interview. The complaint must be a signed statement from the complainant or the complainant's attorney, containing the complainant's (or representative's) telephone number and address, and must be sufficiently precise to identify the complainant and the agency, and describe generally the action or practice which forms the basis of the complaint. 29 C.F.R. Section 1614.106.

Appendix C – Federal EEO Complaint Processing

A complainant may amend a complaint at any time prior to the conclusion of the investigation to include issues or claims like or related to those raised in the complaint. After requesting a hearing, a complainant may file a motion with the AJ to amend a complaint to include issues or claims like or related to those raised in the complaint. 29 C.F.R. Section 1614.106(d).

The agency must acknowledge receipt of the complaint in writing and inform the complainant of the date on which the complaint was filed, of the address of the EEOC office where a request for a hearing should be sent, that the complainant has the right to appeal the agency's final action or dismissal of a complaint, and that the agency must investigate the complaint within 180 days of the filing date. The agency's acknowledgment must also advise the complainant that when a complaint has been amended, the agency must complete the investigation within the earlier of: (1) 180 days after the last amendment to the complaint; or (2) 360 days after the filing of the original complaint. A complainant may request a hearing from an EEOC AJ on the consolidated complaints any time after 180 days from the date of the first filed complaint. 29 C.F.R. Section 1614.106(e).

Dismissals of Complaints

Prior to a request for a hearing, in lieu of accepting a complaint for investigation an agency may dismiss an entire complaint for any of the following reasons: (1) failure to state a claim, or stating the same claim that is pending or has been decided by the agency or the EEOC; (2) failure to comply with the time limits; (3) filing a complaint on a matter that has not been brought to the attention of an EEO counselor and which is not like or related to the matters counseled; (4) filing a complaint which is the basis of a pending civil action, or which was the basis of a civil action already decided by a court; (5) where the complainant has already elected to pursue the matter through either the negotiated grievance procedure or in an appeal to the Merit Systems Protection Board; (6) where the matter is moot or merely alleges a proposal to take a personnel action; (7) where the complainant cannot be located; (8) where the complainant fails to respond to a request to provide relevant information; (9) where the complaint alleges dissatisfaction with the processing of a previously filed complaint; (10) where the complaint is part of a clear pattern of misuse of the EEO process for a purpose other

Appendix C – Federal EEO Complaint Processing

than the prevention and elimination of employment discrimination. 29 C.F.R. Section 1614.107.

If an agency believes that some, but not all, of the claims in a complaint should be dismissed for the above reasons, it must notify the complainant in writing of the rationale for this determination, identify the allegations which will not be investigated, and place a copy of this notice in the investigative file. This determination shall be reviewable by an EEOC AJ if a hearing is requested on the remainder of the complaint, but is not appealable until final action is taken by the agency on the remainder of the complaint. 29 C.F.R. Section 1614.107(b).

Investigations

Investigations are conducted by the respondent agency. The agency must develop an impartial and appropriate factual record upon which to make findings on the claims raised by the complaint. An appropriate factual record is defined in the regulations as one that allows a reasonable fact finder to draw conclusions as to whether discrimination occurred. 29 C.F.R. Section 1614.108(b).

The investigation must be completed within 180 days from the filing of the complaint. A copy of the investigative file must be provided to the complainant, along with a notification that, within 30 days of receipt of the file, the complainant has the right to request a hearing and a decision from an EEOC AJ or may request an immediate final decision from the agency. 29 C.F.R. Section 1614.108(f).

An agency may make an offer of resolution to a complainant who is represented by an attorney at any time after the filing of a complaint, but not later than the date an AJ is appointed to conduct a hearing. An agency may make an offer of resolution to a complaint, represented by an attorney or not, after the parties have received notice than an administrative judge has been appointed to conduct a hearing, but not later than 30 days prior to a hearing.

Such offer of resolution must be in writing and include a notice explaining the possible consequences of failing to accept the offer. If the complainant fails to accept the offer within 30 days of receipt, and the relief awarded in the final decision on the complaint is not more favorable than the offer, then the complainant shall not receive payment

Appendix C – Federal EEO Complaint Processing

from the agency of attorney's fees or costs incurred after the expiration of the 30-day acceptance period. 29 C.F.R. Section 1614.109(c).

Hearings

Requests for hearing must be sent by the complainant to the EEOC office indicated in the agency's acknowledgment letter, with a copy to the agency's EEO office. Within 15 days of receipt of the request for a hearing, the agency must provide a copy of the complaint file to EEOC. The EEOC will then appoint an AJ to conduct a hearing. 29 C.F.R. Section 1614.108(g).

An EEOC AJ may dismiss a complaint for any of the reasons set out above under Dismissals. 29 C.F.R. Section 1614.109(b).

Prior to the hearing, the parties may conduct discovery. The purpose of discovery is to enable a party to obtain relevant information for preparation of the party's case. Each party initially bears their own costs for discovery, unless the AJ requires the agency to bear the costs for the complainant to obtain depositions or any other discovery because the agency has failed to complete its investigation in a timely manner or has failed to adequately investigate the allegations. For a more detailed description of discovery procedures, see EEOC Management Directive 110, Chapter 6.

Agencies provide for the attendance of all employees approved as witnesses by the AJ. Hearings are considered part of the investigative process, and are closed to the public. The AJ conducts the hearing and receives relevant information or documents as evidence. The hearing is recorded and the agency is responsible for paying for the transcripts of the hearing. Rules of evidence are not strictly applied to the proceedings. If the AJ determines that some or all facts are not in genuine dispute, he or she may limit the scope of the hearing or issue a decision without a hearing.

The AJ must conduct the hearing and issue a decision on the complaint within 180 days of receipt by the AJ of the complaint file from the agency. The AJ will send copies of the hearing record, the transcript and the decision to the parties. If an agency does not issue a final order within 40 days of receipt of the AJ's decision, then the decision becomes

Appendix C – Federal EEO Complaint Processing

the final action by the agency in the matter. 29 C.F.R. Section 1614.109(i).

Final Action by Agencies

When an AJ has issued a decision (either a dismissal, a summary judgment decision or a decision following a hearing), the agency must take final action on the complaint by issuing a final order within 40 days of receipt of the hearing file and the AJ's decision. The final order must notify the complainant whether or not the agency will fully implement the decision of the AJ, and shall contain notice of the complainant's right to appeal to EEOC or to file a civil action. If the final order does not fully implement the decision of the AJ, the agency must simultaneously file an appeal with EEOC and attach a copy of the appeal to the final order. 29 C.F.R. Section 1614.110(a).

When an AJ has not issued a decision (i.e., when an agency dismisses an entire complaint under 1614.107, receives a request for an immediate final decision, or does not receive a reply to the notice providing the complainant the right to either request a hearing or an immediate final decision), the agency must take final action by issuing a final decision. The agency's final decision will consist of findings by the agency on the merits of each issue in the complaint. Where the agency has not processed certain allegations in the complaint for procedural reasons set out in 29 C.F.R. Section 1614.107, it must provide the rationale for its decision not to process the allegations. The agency's decision must be issued within 60 days of receiving notification that the complainant has requested an immediate final decision. The agency's decision must contain notice of the complainant's right to appeal to the EEOC, or to file a civil action in federal court. 29 C.F.R. Section 1614.110(b).

Appeals to the EEOC

Several types of appeals may be brought to the EEOC. A complainant may appeal an agency's final action or dismissal of a complaint within 30 days of receipt. 29 C.F.R. Sections 1614.401(a), 1614.402(a).

A grievant may appeal the final decision of the agency, arbitrator or the FLRA on a grievance when an issue of employment discrimination was raised in the grievance procedure. 29 C.F.R. Section 1614.401(d).

Appendix C – Federal EEO Complaint Processing

If the agency's final action and order do not fully implement the AJ's decision, the agency must appeal to the EEOC. 29 C.F.R. Section 1614.110(a); 29 C.F.R. Section 1614.401(b).

A complainant may appeal to the EEOC for a determination as to whether the agency has complied with the terms of a settlement agreement or decision. 29 C.F.R. Section 1614.504(b).

If the complaint is a class action, the class agent or the agency may appeal an AJ's decision accepting or dismissing all or part of the class complaint. A class agent may appeal a final decision on a class complaint. A class member may appeal a final decision on an individual claim for relief pursuant to a finding of class-wide discrimination. Finally, both the class agent or the agency may appeal from an AJ decision on the adequacy of a proposed settlement of a class action. 29 C.F.R. Section 1614.401(c).

Appeals must be filed with EEOC's Office of Federal Operations (OFO). Any statement or brief on behalf of a complainant in support of an appeal must be submitted to OFO within 30 days of filing the notice of appeal. Any statement or brief on behalf of the agency in support of its appeal must be filed within 20 days of filing the notice of appeal. An agency must submit the complaint file to OFO within 30 days of initial notification that the complainant has filed an appeal or within 30 days of submission of an appeal by the agency. Any statement or brief in opposition to an appeal must be submitted to OFO and served on the opposing party within 30 days of receipt of the statement or brief supporting the appeal, or, if no statement or brief supporting the appeal has been filed, within 60 days of receipt of the appeal. 29 C.F.R. Section 1614.403.

EEOC has the authority to draw adverse inferences against a party failing to comply with its appeal procedures or requests for information. 29 C.F.R. Section 1614.404(c).

The decision on an appeal from an agency's final action is based on a de novo review, except that the review of the factual findings in a decision by an AJ is based on a substantial evidence standard of review. 29 C.F.R. Section 1614.405(a).

Appendix C – Federal EEO Complaint Processing

A party may request that EEOC reconsider its decision within 30 days of receipt of the Commission's decision. Such requests are not a second appeal, and will be granted only when the previous EEOC decision involved a clearly erroneous interpretation of material fact or law; or when the decision will have a substantial impact on the policies, practices or operations of the agency. 29 C.F.R. Section 1614.405(b).

The EEOC's decision will be based on a preponderance of the evidence. The decision will also inform the complainant of his or her right to file a civil action.

Civil Actions

Prior to filing a civil action under Title VII of the Civil Rights Act of 1964 or the Rehabilitation Act of 1973, a federal sector complainant must first exhaust the administrative process set out at 29 C.F.R. Part 1614. "Exhaustion" for the purposes of filing a civil action may occur at different stages of the process. The regulations provide that civil actions may be filed in an appropriate federal court: (1) within 90 days of receipt of the final action where no administrative appeal has been filed; (2) after 180 days from the date of filing a complaint if an administrative appeal has not been filed and final action has not been taken; (3) within 90 days of receipt of EEOC's final decision on an appeal; or (4) after 180 days from the filing of an appeal with EEOC if there has been no final decision by the EEOC. 29 C.F.R. Section 1614.408.

Under the Age Discrimination in Employment Act (ADEA), a complainant may proceed directly to federal court after giving the EEOC notice of intent to sue. 29 C.F.R. Section 1614.201. An ADEA complainant who initiates the administrative process in 29 C.F.R. Part 1614 may also file a civil action within the time frames noted above. 29 C.F.R. Section 1614.408.

Under the Equal Pay Act, a complainant may file a civil action within 2 years (3 years for willful violations), regardless of whether he or she has pursued an administrative complaint. 29 C.F.R. Section 1614.409.

Filing a civil action terminates EEOC processing of an appeal. 29 C.F.R. Section 1614.410.

Class Complaints

Appendix C – Federal EEO Complaint Processing

Class complaints of discrimination are processed differently than individual complaints. See 29 C.F.R. Section 1614.204. The employee or applicant who wishes to file a class complaint must first seek counseling and be counseled, just like an individual complaint. However, once counseling is completed the class complaint is not investigated by the respondent agency. Rather, the complaint is forwarded to the nearest EEOC Field or District Office, where an EEOC AJ is appointed to make decision as to whether to accept or dismiss the class complaint. The AJ examines the class to determine whether it meets the class certification requirements of numerosity, commonality, typicality and adequacy of representation. The AJ may issue a decision dismissing the class because it fails to meet any of these class certification requirements, as well as for any of the reasons for dismissal discussed above for individual complaints (see section 5, above).

A class complaint may begin as an individual complaint of discrimination. At a certain point, it may become evident that there are many more individuals than the complainant affected by the issues raised in the individual complaint. EEOC's regulations provide that a complainant may move for class certification at any reasonable point in the process when it becomes apparent that there are class implications to the claims raised in an individual complaint. 29 C.F.R. Section 1614.204(b).

The AJ transmits his or her decision to accept or dismiss a class complaint to the class agent and the agency. The agency must then take final action by issuing a final order within 40 days of receipt of the AJ's decision. The final order must notify the agent whether or not the agency will implement the decision of the AJ. If the agency's final order does not implement the AJ's decision, the agency must simultaneously appeal the AJ's decision to EEOC's OFO. A copy of the agency's appeal must be appended to the agency's final order. 29 C.F.R. Section 1614.204(d)(7).. A dismissal of a class complaint shall inform the class agent either that the complaint is being filed on that date as an individual complaint and processed accordingly, or that the complaint is also dismissed as an individual complaint for one of the reasons for dismissal (discussed in section E, above). In addition, a dismissal must inform the class agent of the right to appeal to EEOC's OFO or to file a civil action in federal court.

Appendix C – Federal EEO Complaint Processing

When a class complaint is accepted, the agency must use reasonable means to notify the class members of the acceptance of the class complaint, a description of the issues accepted as part of the complaint, an explanation of the binding nature of the final decision or resolution on the class members, and the name, address and telephone number of the class representative. 29 C.F.R. Section 1614.204(e). In lieu of an investigation by the respondent agency, an EEOC AJ develops the record through discovery and a hearing. The AJ then issues a recommended decision to the agency. Within 60 days of receipt of the AJ's recommended decision on the merits of the class complaint, the agency must issue a final decision which either accepts, rejects or modifies the AJ's recommended decision. If the agency fails to issue such a decision within that time frame, the AJ's recommended decision becomes the agency's final decision in the class complaint.

When discrimination is found in the final decision and a class member believes that he or she is entitled to relief, the class member may file a written claim with the agency within 30 days of receipt of notification by the agency of its final decision. The EEOC AJ retains jurisdiction over the complaint in order to resolve disputed claims by class members. The claim for relief must contain a specific showing that the claimant is a class member entitled to relief. EEOC's regulations provide that, when a finding of discrimination against a class has been made, there is a presumption of discrimination as to each member of the class. The agency must show by clear and convincing evidence that any class member is not entitled to relief. The agency must issue a final decision on each individual claim for relief within 90 days of filing. Such decision may be appealed to EEOC's OFO, or a civil action may be filed in federal court. 29 C.F.R. Section 1614.204(l)(3).

A class complaint may be resolved at any time by agreement between the agency and the class agent. Notice of such resolution must be provided to all class members, and reviewed and approved by an EEOC AJ. If the AJ finds that the proposed resolution is not fair to the class as a whole, the AJ will issue a decision vacating the agreement, and may replace the class agent with some other eligible class member to further process the class complaint. Such decision may be appealed to EEOC. If the AJ finds that the resolution is fair to the class as a whole, the resolution is binding on all class members. 29 C.F.R. Section 1614.204(g).

Appendix C – Federal EEO Complaint Processing

Grievances

Persons covered by collective bargaining agreements which permit allegations of discrimination to be raised in the grievance procedure, and who wish to file a complaint or grievance on an allegation of employment discrimination, must elect to proceed either under the procedures of 29 C.F.R. Part 1614 or the negotiated grievance procedures, but not both. 29 C.F.R. Section 1614.301(a). An election to proceed under Part 1614 is made by the filing of a complaint, and an election to proceed under the negotiated grievance procedures is made by filing a grievance. Participation in the pre-complaint procedures of Part 1614 is not an election of the 1614 procedures. The election requirement does not apply to employees of agencies not covered by 5 U.S.C. Section 7121(d), notably employees of the United States Postal Service.

Mixed Case Complaints

Some employment actions which may be the subject of a discrimination complaint under Part 1614 may also be appealed to the Merit Systems Protection Board (MSPB). In such cases, the employee must elect to proceed with a complaint as a "mixed case complaint" under Part 1614, or a "mixed case appeal" before the MSPB. Whichever is filed first is considered an election to proceed in that forum. 29 C.F.R. Section 1614.302.

Mixed case complaints are processed similarly to other complaints of discrimination, with the following notable exceptions: (1) the agency has only 120 days from the date of the filing of the mixed case complaint to issue a final decision, and the complainant may appeal the matter to the MSPB or file a civil action any time thereafter; (2) the complainant must appeal the agency's decision to the MSPB, not the EEOC, within 30 days of receipt of the agency's decision; (3) at the completion of the investigation the complainant does not have the right to request a hearing before an EEOC AJ, and the agency must issue a decision within 45 days. 29 C.F.R. Section 1614.302(d).

Individuals who have filed either a mixed case complaint or a mixed case appeal, and who have received a final decision from the MSPB, may petition the EEOC to review the MSPB final decision.

Appendix C – Federal EEO Complaint Processing

In contrast to non-mixed matters, individuals who wish to file a civil action in mixed- case matters must file within 30 days (not 90) of receipt of: (1) the agency's final decision; (2) the MSPB's final decision; or (3) the EEOC's decision on a petition to review. Alternatively, a civil action may be filed after 120 days from the date of filing the mixed case complaint with the agency or the mixed case appeal with the MSPB if there has been no final decision on the complaint or appeal, or 180 days after filing a petition to review with EEOC if there has been no decision by EEOC on the petition. 29 C.F.R. Section 1614.310.

Other Publications by Joseph Swerdzewski

THE ESSENTIAL GUIDE TO FEDERAL LABOR RELATIONS ~ What you need to know to be successful

The Essential Guide to Federal Labor Relations gives your Managers, Supervisors, Labor Relations Practitioners, and Union Representatives an in-depth understanding of labor relations concepts. This easy to read comprehensive guide is essential for practitioners and those actively involved in day-to-day labor relations.

LABOR LAW AND LABOR RELATIONS 5th Edition – A Practical Guide to Federal Labor Relations

The 5th Edition of Labor Law and Labor Relations has been updated to help you understand the law even better. It is an easy to read practical guide that every manager, supervisor, and union steward who spends 25% of their time on Labor Relations needs to have, in order to understand their role in Federal Sector Labor Relations! This is a practical guide to federal labor relations and does not attempt to explain the intricacies of the complex federal system but instead gives federal supervisors, working managers and union representatives a general understanding of what they need to know to be effective in labor relations.

A Guide to Successful Federal Sector Collective Bargaining

Everything Managers, Supervisors, and Union Representatives need to know about Collective Bargaining in the Federal Sector!

Here is a partial list of topics covered: Federal Sector Bargaining Processes, Duty to Bargain, Scope of Bargaining, Procedures and Appropriate Arrangements, The Change Bargaining Process, Ground Rules for Bargaining, Preparation for Bargaining, Language in a Collective Bargaining Agreement, Official Time, Alternative Work Schedules, How to Negotiate, and Relationship of the Parties.

COMMUNICATION AND TRUST ~ A GUIDE TO A SUCCESSFUL WORK PLACE

This book is sure to help Managers, Employees, and Union Representatives everywhere build better relationships in the work place.
Learn to develop more effective communication skills!
Learn how communication and trust work hand-in-hand in the workplace.
Read real life workplace scenarios where communication went wrong and learn what to do in similar situations.

HOW TO CONDUCT A WORKPLACE INVESTIGATION

Everything your Managers, Supervisors, Union Representatives, and Lawyers need to know about workplace investigations! Here is a partial list of topics covered: The Investigator's Authority, Common Problems of Investigators, Developing an Investigative Plan, Investigator Communication Skills, Evidence, Conduct and Role of an Investigator, Preparation for an Investigation, Interviewing and/or Questioning Witnesses, Witness Right and Representation, and Investigative Reports.

Made in the USA
Columbia, SC
20 April 2020